DEAR APOCALYPSE

DEAR APOCALYPSE

K. A. HAYS

CARNEGIE MELLON UNIVERSITY PRESS
PITTSBURGH 2009

ACKNOWLEDGMENTS

I would like to thank the editors of the following journals, in which these poems, some in altered form, have appeared:

AGNI Online: "Exodus"
Antioch Review: "The Way of All the Earth"
Black Warrior Review: "Serotinous"
Cincinnati Review: "Expulsion," "Here"
Florida Review: "The Labor of Waking," "That Death"
Gray's Sporting Journal: "Not Like Ghosts but Like the White Robes Worn"
Greensboro Review: "Outside the Basilica di San Petronio"
The Literary Review: "Arrival"
Mid-American Review: "I Made My Soul a Hat"
The Missouri Review: "I Don't Believe the View from Here," "I'd Say God,"
    "Dear Apocalypse," "So the Moths Come Slaloming Out of Hollow Trees"
    "The Churchbells in Malé Are Ringing, Possibly Ushering Out"
New Orleans Review: "Letter from the End of the World," "Meanwhile," "Sacrament,"
    "This Morning After Snow, the Body Scrapes Off," "Leap," "In the
    Garden," "The Snow Queen Speaks of April," "The Ice Festival"
Notre Dame Review: "Conversion," "Letter from the Afternoon," "The Sea Clots
    Whitely After the Swell, Claws Sand"
Poet Lore: "But Then Again It Might Be Possible"
Subtropics: "It Is Easy Not to See the Mad"
Southern Humanities Review: "Hyacinths" (as "Dark Work"), "Genesis"
Southern Poetry Review: "Theology"
the Southern Review: "Pastoral"

"Serotinous" was reprinted in *Best New Poets 2007*, ed. Natasha Trethewey. "Sacrament" was reprinted on the website Poetry Daily, December 28, 2007. I am most grateful to Katie Ford, whose keen editorial vision helped this book to reach its final form; to Paula Closson Buck and Deirdre O'Connor for their responses as early readers; to Bucknell's Stadler Center for Poetry, and its director Shara McCallum, for generous support in the form of the Emerging Writer Fellowship; and to the teachers whose delight in and knowledge of literature and poetry deepened mine: Nancy Robinson, Karen Mapes, Harold Schweizer, Joshua Harmon, John Haines, David Bradshaw, Robert Love Taylor, John Rickard, Arnold Weinstein, Carole Maso, Brian Evenson, and others. Finally, to my parents, Camilla Tassone Hays and Robert Hays, who showed me the joy and solace of the arts, and to a still greater joy and solace, my husband Andrew Ciotola—my love and thanks.

Book design: Julie Brown, Elliot Smith, Caitlinn Cork

The publication of this book is made possible by a grant from the Pennsylvania Council on the Arts.

PENNSYLVANIA
COUNCIL
ON THE
ARTS

Library of Congress Control Number 200892386
ISBN 978-0-88748-495-7

Printed and bound in the United States of America

10 9 8 7 6 5 4 3 2 1

for my parents
and for Andy

CONTENTS

DEAR APOCALYPSE

DEAR APOCALYPSE

Gust through—   good. Give us

over to the oaks,   sway the old

sheds, the mansions—   shake them down

to meadows,   unmake us, melt off

what was wasted   of our waking years—

but know   we're no worse

than former fools.   You could have felled us

a millennium back,   blasted and bludgeoned—

you're late.   Level us, but let it be

put in stone   (or penciled on plastic):

Here lie some bodies   who bear no blame

for any faults   the future may find

at rest in their ruins.   Remember: we had

a god who grumbled   through us, gave us

his face, held us—   fisted, we like to feel—

even as he ended us.   Excuse him.

He was, like any other man,   complicated.

I. LETTERS

What if this present were the world's last night?

—John Donne

LETTER FROM THE END OF THE WORLD

They must have wearied of looking in on us,

the meridians. They shook the earth's rugs

and broke away. Now we must be like saints,

barefoot and flexible. We ache for the years we fought

for our gods, before this wind

began playing our landmarks, felling

our churches, mosques, synagogues, lobbing

the bricks and stones skyward. It is terrible,

we say in every language

as it spins down homes and schools

and juggles the ruins—.

We wail like children on the beach

who had intended the slow spoil of a city

of sand, but were slighted by the sea

flinging through too soon. Too soon:

Meridians, you who guided and lulled us,

we accuse you.

Your spines left circular runnels

in the sky, through which we can see the great arbiter,

as bland and ready as a cast-iron pan—in whose image

we fear, squinting, we were not made.

MEANWHILE

All of us, every one,

will be dissolved not long from now.

Meanwhile we tuck away the winter's claims,

put photos in a box, look elsewhere.

It is not as difficult as it would seem

to shrug off the dead. Half the population

could go in fires—ah, we would say, but look,

the snowdrops hang their brows

beneath the shrubs, a sign of spring!

And the winged insects, hatching.

There will be a disasters special

on the news tonight—we will mourn then.

Now the grackles have returned.

I hear their hideous clacking

as they slam about in packs, settling

in the stripped branches—moving

as if an equation, perfect. That is how

we must live: mathematically,

like seedlings in the shade of the old ash,

waiting for rot, when we will fight

for a place to grow.

LETTER FROM THE AFTERNOON

One assumes the universe
slags on with its business,
though it seems to have wearied of late
and only that monster, the cane begonia,
with jagged leaves like the wings of vultures,
hurries up to the windows overlooking the street.

It doesn't bother with this room
or its shelves of books.
It ignores the gold embossing
on their spines. We reach for them—
crushing, how unlike them we are—
our titles clashing with our plots,
bits of narration missing or absurd.
More saddening is the thought of after,

when this stint is done and some other species
stomps and sings here. Of course there will be no one
to read our ruins—only some bugs who have no sense
of the tragic. Some think after our extinction
earth might be calm—but I doubt it.
The begonia, with its red undersides
and sly roots, hulks on, an ordinary zealot,
shading out the philodendron, hoarding sun.

IN THE GARDEN

Afternoons past three o'clock, the orchard shrugs.

The unripe apples look jaded and the air

tastes like fruit fermented. Afternoons

make us listless things, overripe. Why is it?

And soon the rattler, tomorrow, will swallow us,

its skin first gold, then brown, then shed. . . . Pluck,

heave me away to the compost. Afternoons I need

to talk epistemology with something ugly

and inanimate: the earth, for example.

PASTORAL

August, swift-fisted with heat, uppercuts me

and leaves, as apology, corn. Cob and husk

I bury, pluck the kernels for false teeth

and grin, bogus as crop circles. Someone's burning

poison ivy. Here the smoke is a wet quilt

hung out in morning. Often I want

to wrap up in it and lie still. Even now

the farmer is rolling large, inedible pumpkins

from the patch, humming Taps. Autumn

aches here. Throbs. Even the churches smell

of hay, the sermons go yellow

under the preacher's tongue, my prayers

waddle off, claim they need a purpose

beyond the tradition. I understand. The faithful

have forked tongues; Indian corn gleams darkly

from their lips, making them difficult

to take seriously. Only the worms loop on

with confidence, poking up from the earth, the blissful

gods of mud (the maker of man). They bring

the dung and fouled leaves through their bodies.

I smell their castings even in the burrows I dig

at two A.M. and curl in, hoping to wake

rose-tinged, translucent, devolved.

SEROTINOUS

We should learn from them: the copse

of pitch pines leaning into a mohawk, all needle

and warted twig. If someone lit a blaze out here,

they wouldn't blink. They have,

in fact, grown dormant buds

made to open in such terror. Good idea for us

to fashion, like them, root collars—

so if the body cooked to the nub, buds gone,

another self might climb out, cough, unfold greenly—

though safer still, for the populace,

to be schooled in serotinous cones,

to learn to lock our seed in a resin

that melts off only in fire,

so if the bud and root and trunk

are cooked, the seeds are saved, and spring

from the charred earth after the dumb maples and oaks,

with their studied aesthetics of leaf and even shade,

samaras and acorns, have gone.

The pitch pines welter, clawed on ledges

with their roots in near-rock,

fed by the ground's toxic metals. Remember—

if not for the arbitrary crash that startled off

a piece of the planet, forming the moon

and tilting the earth off-kilter,

there would be none of us. Convenient,

that we have this creator in us,

erratic. Poised to burn.

THE ICE FESTIVAL

Night and the air hums septic orange

over the round path in the park

where we shuffle, murmuring from thin coats—

disappointment. All day we waited

behind closed windows, not needing to hear

the clanks haranguing, the artists chiseling

through sultry noon, cutting what the town ordered

in defiance of thaw. We are here for beauty,

our procession—but have only the ruined shapes,

the empty pedestals, substance split

over grass, downed silvery and mud-stricken,

white shards caught in the chaos

of their falling. Here, the inchoate depictions.

Here what the artists wanted runs into the slur

of grass and puddle that floods our steps.

At the entrance stands the centerpiece—four hearts

hollowed and connected, carved
of hundred-pound blocks, a hazardous feat

that slows the crowd. I want this to give us
any clean, proud grace we had come for,

the confident weight of well-carved cold; yet
the hearts whisper cracks. Everyone hears

their shudder, blue fissures feeding through
the skin spidered networks. It has rounded. It drips

colossally, our festival, our ice. We cluster, close.
This is not love's triumph. This is not art

refining nature. No old theme we love.
This is—grim, sullied—how soon passes

the ideal we had imagined, how it won't wait
for our coming, won't pause at the wake

of our need. And how imminent, for each of us
and for our way of knowing, a spectacular crash.

II.   LABORS

That was when the ones who smiled
Were the dead.

—Anna Akhmatova

THE WAY OF ALL THE EARTH

Joshua 23:14

In various ways we'll be taken. Fine, except
that we know it, and just when we've tricked it away
someone nearby—a sister, say, or a child—proves it again
as fact. More pleasant to be one of those turtles
who each September takes a last breath
and goes gliding down to the profound mud
to wag in for a fine six months of anti-meditation.
How brown it would be,
and more than milky, an opaque shell
around the shell of the body, any minnow who passed
taking the body for rocks that had sat on the bottom
for centuries, mossing. We would not attend
the last rites of our families. We would be happy
as stone until spring when we swam upwards
to catch ducks in our snappers—
oh, unavoidable affront, especially
for the old, for whom death's quick mouth
darts daily through reed and shallow pool.
It snatches from the surface the children
and sleek teens of the past, each month a volley
of funerals, leading up to the snap over a webbed foot,
when the self, which quakes and rages, is dragged under
until it is drowned. Better, perhaps, not to go
alone, but to pile, instead, like other turtles
on top of one another in a river's trench—

to stay alive by being nearly dead.

When the winter of dust

blustered sixty-four million years back,

and the great beasts who stalked the land suffered

and fell, their bulk heaving the hills—

all of that was only a loud game of billiards

to the turtles, who sank down away from the light

and let the arms and legs float in the waters,

each belly atop another shell, the skin assuming

the work of the lungs, so the lungs—

as the earth above wasted and tore—

might, through that din, be still.

THAT DEATH

That death I remember
as I remember the brush wolf
at dusk along the woods road. It loped,

a line no longer than a hyphen,
and skimmed the scrub a half mile off,
then sat, to make a silhouette

of dog (but not quite dog). I sensed
what it was, but did not want to come
to the fact (to touch the rib, to rub

the raked fur at the crown). It stood, all legs,
low tail trailing after, then thralled off
into the laurel. I remember how the gum trees

looked that day, blushing
in unison. It was August. The air
was not yet cold. There was, and is,

a privacy about the thing
that suspends one until it trots off.
To the mind. Or wherever the dead go.

THE SNOW QUEEN SPEAKS OF APRIL

In the long months, the cold has lips

like a burn nothing can soothe.

It carries chains. The cold rubs up

to night and coaxes it to bed,

claims it. I know the need—to slip

a sheet over the passive buds,

to bludgeon the thyme and slow

the juncos. Look, the seedlings

curtsy, shy under their garlands, and sleet

gives stinging keyboard clicks, working

to make coherent the ivy, the dormant

crab grass. The chimes hang unswaying,

as if the Romans built them. I want to see

as a garden would, in winter: the toad

under leaves, mapped in brown,

a fine and perfect art. Soon he will heat

and hunger, dig out to sing, mate

messily in April. I don't love the cold,

but it knows me. If I went to it and stood,

it would make of me what I want to find elsewhere—

an exhibit. Held, if on the verge of being lost.

AFTER LOSS

Here lavish sprays of deer piss stain the snow.

Also the holes a buck must have dug

just by walking, sinking past his ankles,

at each base the split-heart of his hoof.

For the buck there was no after, no care

for prints or evidence, only in, and in, and in—.

THE CHURCHBELLS IN MALÉ ARE RINGING, POSSIBLY USHERING OUT

the last of the funeral goers I passed on my way

to these foothills. From here I can see the stone bell tower

and the Dolomite-flanked park where a girl is crying.

The beetles in these hills wear painted masks

and move like prayers in every direction.

The bells seem intent on some kind of valediction.

I have no names for the wildflowers here.

Their perfume is like wood. No one is expecting me home.

HYACINTHS

I.

They are not to be touched,
say the instructions, "Hyacinths in Forcing Vases"—

their crystals leave a rash on sensitive skin.
The three bulbs look like ancient kiln-fired balls:

dry, mottled, blue and purple—some kind of anti-Easter eggs
to suggest not a rise from the dead, but a fall

from the living. I wear gloves,
balance each bulb on its vase of water. Almost touching,

but not. A bulb will rot in water,
so it must sit, hanging over

what could end it. I am to leave my bulbs alone.
They are doing their dark work.

II.

At the back of the closet where it is cold
as window glass, but less transparent,

they cannot know how long it will take.

They will go into a season of night

and come out, supposedly, with leaves and roots, robust,
ready for spring. Weekly I reach behind the sweaters.

My bulbs appall me. Two of them, though brief on top,
are thrusting hungrily, angrily downwards,

flinging dense tangles of growth
into the water, as if they want to bury themselves

in that still nether-region where sounds are muted.
What could come of such inwardness?

Of such thin ghosts?

III.

I don't know when the bloom of them will come,
have never had hyacinths, am finding books,
am reading there will be monstrous flowers—
strange, blue, many in one, belled, harsh, thick,

no frail things, not easily torn. I am learning my blooms

will have black markings, which the Greeks translate

as *ai ai*, an expression of grief.

IV.

My third bulb refuses to send out shoots.

It is stubborn. It clings

to the surface, paltry base succinct

as stubble. It will not be moved by a false winter.

Soon, when two bulbs have lifted

an inch of green into the air and floated

half-foot threads in water, my third bulb

smells of fish left in boats,

the mice who crawl into the ducts.

I throw it in the garbage disposal.

With a grind it sends up its stench, its last cry.

The others go on, now raising pale cupped hands

in the closet, as if their submerged appendages

have given them the strength to grow

upwards to a light that isn't there.

DARKLING

From the laurel past its flower,

evening coming on, cloud mass sodden and curt,

the thrush flutes first three minor notes,

                then answers them

in lower register, a stillborn music sorrowing out,

echoing back, then falling off as if

the century, a bleak anaphora, were done.

                The dog stands with me,

then wags down-trail to a carcass, most likely,

in which she will roll, ecstatic as churchgoers

slain by the spirit. I want to see the bird that makes

                these sounds. If this is the music

of a soul out-flung, well—it's a wretched thing

Hardy heard. And now the thrush flaps down,

freckled and tan, abrupt

                as the undead. It perches

on a stump and calls a warning note at me.

The dog trots back. She's brining in slaver

a puttied thing, bloodied, small-winged:

                a tiny thrush. So—

the mother thrush wings off. Surely

she has lost countless fledglings. For her

these departures must be

                          as common as dusk,

as old as the sense that we, living,

might be excused from this.

EXODUS

As was forecast, the windows hold the fingerprints

that blotted them yesterday; the fence keeps

each plank at attention; the chimneys usher through

the ghost of wood. On certain days I'd hope

for the bricks to thump out of their mortar, primed

for a higher course; for the porch pillars to stalk off

their platforms, shrugging at the collapse; for any mass

rebellion of the quiet functioning things. Instead,

the juncos wallow and thrash in gutters all over town,

even in my gutters, with their holes larger than eye sockets

weeping wet rust. Like a great plot, the pipes and wires push,

the pavement trills with our going, the street signs point everyone

silently and usefully onward. I'd be on my way, walking barefoot

toward the coast, but who would ferry my boat?

Would it have low gunnels? a lost oar? a little seat at the bow?

Is that how I'd know it was mine?

THE LABOR OF WAKING

Difficult work. For the man who falls out

of mass migrations, waking

to a cot in Kazakhstan, for the woman who can wed

sleep as salt weds water

but rises for the graveyard shift, for all six billion of us

meandering wakers, tongues

ballooned beyond speech, seeing in sleep

a side of things more greenly,

where a room's wrought

in bolder hues, and seethes with meaning, it is difficult.

Of course, we must pretend

it is easy, must cast off our starred coverlets

as if they were nets, flop out

onto the cold floor. We must not unsettle

the dog, we must not cry—

though there was a first waking, a tumbling and splitting

where we were permitted to show

the gut urge, our hatred for being here.

Then we had purple faces,

clenched fists, closed eyes, the most perfect wail.

To give back an honesty to things

we would, the six billion of us, each day wake with the visible

signs of our horror, slick

with the fluids of elsewhere—and dream, a great placenta,

would fall out with us, baggy

and black, deflated on the floor.

Some spirit of good would swab and dress

our bodies, would take photographs:

the puckered lips, the dark tomato faces,

our wrinkles, little nowheres

from the nowhere we'd been.

We would gurgle, not yet knowing

those valleys where many walk,

the pits into which the awakened fall,

that there will come so many terrors to us

and to our measured hours.

Or that, after many mornings, many days,

we would come to love

this waking life enough to dread its loss.

III. MIND

Hands, do what you're bid:
Bring the balloon of the mind
That bellies and drags in the wind
Into its narrow shed.

—W. B. Yeats

BUT THEN AGAIN IT MIGHT BE POSSIBLE

that it is like the winter wren in the cavity

of the hemlock, looking out. Or like boiling

water poured to loose tea, which takes on,

as it steeps, a peppery gold clairvoyance.

It may be that the soul is not

a sham, that the body hosts some animal

we haven't seen, but sense rooting

uneasily through us. The faithful

have said it for millennia, true—but

I see the news and think

there's only that sexed-up, thick-petalled

orchid that flings itself off a wilted stem.

Grotesque balloon, the brain. And why

so unacceptable, in death, to heave off

consciousness, which gives the sense of being

a cut wire, buzzing in the grass? To lose

that burden and be, say, a spoon—something

that doesn't care, but is, and helps—I wouldn't mind it.

Or else I would. I've read the wren has a double

voice, halftones and overtones, released

in the same moment. I think of doubting

and believing, a failed duet,

the mind, that mousy bird that nests

in tangled growth. We want to end the thing

and all its troubled sounds—and we want it to stay.

I DON'T BELIEVE THE VIEW FROM HERE

Of course, somewhere else the sea goes nodding

and rolling its eyes, gossiping with the gulls,

their cackle and dip conspiratorial. No doubt

somewhere farther out than anyone swims,

the whales comb the waters with their baleen.

How easy it would be

if I had a filter like that for perception,

so only, say, honeydew and the words of true prophets

could rush in like nourishing plankton while my own death

and the suffering of others couldn't reach me

but were stopped just at the lip—

But there is more to it.

Here the ground bees funnel up from their burrows.

A thousand slip from a thousand holes, each scrapping

firm soil for a bunker she builds by herself, and lives in alone.

This one is spinning from her mouth a waterproof sac

she'll fill with pollen and an egg. No one will see into that home

while the bee is still swelling. No one will peer into a burrow

to see how he hatches or what he does at night,

whether he grooms himself or nestles into leaves,

whether he senses the sea—.

IT IS EASY NOT TO SEE THE MAD

radiance in the alley, the chicory's violet

gaze above the spangled glass

and gravel. It is best to miss,

as well, the worms, spent scabs

sun-fried, reminiscent of—

      but better not to reminisce.

Morning and only one weed

shocks the ground. Only in morning it blooms

like any other soul, with grim lucidity,

and it could split the sky like fruit

to peel its skin back, though chicory

wants no more than what it is. It lets

      the day gasp through. It lifts

its face. Edged by the terror of asphalt, the bulk

of anthills fallen and mangled feathers, bugs

crushed, scum, piss, the chicory keeps its difficult

poise. Morning. Slim stems snaking up. The sun

careening higher until it accuses,

strips off shadows. The petals close—

it's true—from too much day.

IMAGINE HOW EASY IT MUST BE FOR WEATHER

It's enough to curdle some jealousy in we humans—

saying we're fine, as dull

as blue skies in children's drawings,

white space between us and the spiky grass—

it's a shame we couldn't choke the worms out of the mud

as signs to one another, little hints.

And now the worms wallow up, ridiculous

as the insane, who have permission to go naked.

Surely we all fear the reach of madness.

But what if it made us as confident as the wind billowing

a hurricane, far past the flat snare of beaches,

over the triangle where ships go off radar

and laws get sucked down?

Let's say we could cook in the slurried waves,

spitting out the brack in us,

permitting what's necessary. Imagine that:

doing what conditions urge.

THE SEA CLOTS WHITELY AFTER
THE SWELL, CLAWS SAND

Tonight Draco rises in the northeast over this.

I can trace the dragon's shape,

pinned up there, the ordered anarchy of its stars.

Draco used to roam around crippling humans

until Athena bristled, took the beast by his tail

      and swung him so he spiraled

around the polestar and stayed. A comfort—to think

that chaos rolls its eyes back light years from here

because reason raised her arm—though

even now these bodiless pincers and spiny shells

keep washing to my feet. I pick one up

      and hurl it, watch the long arc starwards,

pleased with my throw for a moment before it drops

to the sea, which keeps bellying up to me

cold-blooded, crushing what it can.

I MADE MY SOUL A HAT

Plaid, tasseled, it caught, I guess, some honey

locust along the curb. Or it was taken

by a wind, as I often am, and its wool,

which only sometimes itched my brow,

fainted over a branch. I must have schlepped on

unchanged, witless as ever. It is not indispensable,

after all, but simple to forget—

though this one I wanted,

as it recalled my father's Scottish side.

A week later I found it, crowning

a parking meter. Someone must have wrung it

from the puddle or street into which it had blown,

decided it had an owner who might come

looking. I wasn't—but wondered. What if each hat

along the gutter were another lost self? And the old

knit hats that fester, abandoned, mud-spun

along the curb—what if we picked them up

and tried them on? Conflicting, to collect and wear

the strays, the toques and balaclavas, the stiff

spent fleece—would it make us schizophrenic,

or just lonely? What is the soul

if not what helps us feel detached? A voice?

No, we must make the soul

a single hat,

a wool-acrylic blend, worn only privately,

slipped over the eyes to shut out street lights.

What loftier purpose for the obsolete spirit,

but to be, lint-caught and pilled,

an insulating dome, giving the sense of distance

from our too-lit rooms, ubiquitous wars—

a hat. Pull it lower. Lower still.

GENESIS

The ocean chafed and slashed when I was four,
of course. The sand smoldered and the rocks
bladed pools that filled and drained. The hub

of all this wonder, I hunched over the coquinas—mollusks
the size of a toenail—digging and laying them out
along the bruise of sea. I made them sun-glossed, perfect.

They fought my will, shone nakedly, snaked down.
It thrilled me, their insistence—that a being with only a foot
could want and believe in someplace after here,

choosing to leave the whip of sun and churn of breakers,
headed somewhere freer, darker.
I took up my shovel. I idled away.

EXPULSION

Now my stirrup hoe sweeps, troubles the weeds,

evicts them from their ground, inverted scythe

quicker and purer than head-chopping, grieving

over no tendril, missing no scrap that might

push back out of the dirt. Up here the bed

scowls, an ugly country parched and wind-plied

as any of us. Grumbling, the pale-red

light snarls through. It herds the hoe

back to its shed, as if some god wanted

me out—wringing the swath of dun-clouds over

the garden, making rain. Almost a relief

to take again a passive stance, to go

sit idle at the edge of it, feeling

the mind, fragile, just uprooted, arrive

in a new cold. Drink. And take leave.

THAT BELLIES AND DRAGS

Here houses insist on one story
and one story only—as if height

would smudge them into the too-real
sky, that deranged persona who sees

what falls and wanders, and what grows.
Nuthatches dart on the undersides of branches,

watching oaks sprout from green clouds
and clouds climb from treetops,

not knowing the accurate view,
nothing being constant but stones,

which are scattered, kicked, hurled.
They break what they did not ask to break.

Puncture tires without decision.
The gutters slump everywhere,

letting themselves fill with leaf
and slime and things that crawl.

I remember feeling that kind of acceptance.

Letting everything in, my mind since hoping

to be stone, then ranch house,

though, I admit, it is mostly nuthatch.

I want what lives but doesn't change—

a cliché, only because the whole earth wants this.

Even the mold on bread, even that

wants to stay mold, to see the room always

as mold does, however that is, upside down

or through a dark glass. Or not at all.

THIS MORNING AFTER SNOW,
THE BODY SCRAPES OFF

sludge, is mere action. It strips the sleet from the walk

at dawn, blue-lit, forging a path as water would,

with that constant stream of spite for solids, whose fixed

contented stupor everyone wants. A pain—

that we're mostly water and therefore subject

to the flaws liquid has, in addition to the joke

of being aware. Best, if we can manage it,

to annul thought—to hunch frozen, ground-bent

and sure as bullies, fixing the brow as if

a thread were drawn from leaf rot to face,

sewn up to the fickle air. Best, after too much

vision, to be only might—an organizing

grunt, a mass. Gutted. Shoveling corewards.

IV.   FOWLS AND LILIES

They toil not, neither do they spin.

—Matthew 6:28

Brooding on God, I may become a man.

—Theodore Roethke

OUTSIDE THE BASILICA DI SAN PETRONIO

A girl is after pigeons, tracking them.
She bows her head. She holds up her palms.
Her hand goes out and the things gust off.

Meanwhile the nuns in the basilica clutch beads
beneath their habits. And the priest
cleans the chalice, making it shine.

She is eager for the next step: to hold the flurry
of beak and breast, to draw it close.
She is stepping, pausing, tensed
and watchful as the underside of prayer.

When the birds rise, the white in their breasts
flashes before the basilica. The girl's arms fall.
It is as easy as wine to blood, how they lift
into the ether. They are as good to her

as the miraculous saints. Dear saints,
keeping always and perfectly away.

SOME PIGEONS AMBLE BY THE TRACKS

unfazed when the train pours through.

In the vineyards here, the vines lean on pergolas,

hail nets draped over, drifting up.

A woman walks the rows, the buds she's tending

far from grapes, farther still from wine.

When the train lags, the poppies by the station

bend flush with the ground, then right themselves.

It's as if faith were as easy as that:

re-tilting the red faces, lifting up the stems.

LETTER FROM CINQUE TERRE

They've tied a net between two olive trees

and rolled it up for when the olives get

mature and suicidal, any breeze

reason enough to call it quits—to let

the whole ripening business go to rot.

They'd drop dramatically off, the end—except,

of course, for the plan to harvest and cure the lot

of bitterness. I'd say we're more like trees

than olives, anyway—reliable, caught

and letting continuously go, forgetting what's gone

and bowed by storms, watching belief, a net,

flail and twist, while the trunk stays false-stoically on.

THEOLOGY

The sea, for now, is a blue swag
on the land's shelf. The gulls hold out
their wings to catch gusts, hover, swoop,
pick fish off the water—I will not come too close
to see the fish wide-eyed as they're eaten.

I'd rather enjoy the white feathers on the blue,
safe as embroidery. I am doing for the gulls
what a god would do for us: standing outside.

I am squinting; I am smiling at the distant shapes.
The woman at the shoreline in a red suit
bends to cup the water over her knees.

She is washing off sand. The red of suit,
the flex of arm, the blue of sea—
why should there be a god?

Next to the woman is a rusted pipe
that brought in sand to make a larger shoreline—
good. We adults spread out. We sniff the breeze
as a toddler wails and rubs his eyes. All over the beach

we rub our eyes silently, shed sandy tears,

squint, blink at the gulls. Better not to cry out.

We have learned, sitting here, doing

what the dependable gods would have done,

that wailing will do little good. The day is fine.

SACRAMENT

And the hectic show of birds rewinds

and plays itself endlessly, loops, rallies through

this warped and baffling film we call the real.

What perfect closeness they have, circling

the chimneys, pillaring down—it seems surprising

        when out of that sifting

a swift breaks itself on a window, folds to the road,

the sun as brilliant as a steel can. The seconds

skip on, unflagged, and the grass gives itself to the seeded

wildness it wants to become. What does it mean

when a swift comes to eat its own dead? To be safe,

        we must jeer at the birds,

they are so different. To them we are only alien

flesh, a smell that moves in the brush.

As one, they bob on the air's tides. It is as if

they had divine purpose, as if we were second

to them—as untroubling as the stars. Philistines.

        I want that kind of communion.

SO THE MOTHS COME SLALOMING
OUT OF HOLLOW TREES

as do the butterflies, the so-called spring azures,

a brilliant confetti falling, swung up

and sailing,

       fending off the swift parabolas

of birds, who hunt but fail to catch

that odd, incorporeal blue. The magnolia,

who held for months her buds

in gray down coats, now lets

their skin peek out,

       blushed, vestal—

what's on its way? The coltsfoot seems poised to exhale

when an April snow flops down, muting it. The azures,

who overwintered, anyway,

       just for these three days,

just to lay eggs in spring, expire. Really,

only the mourning cloaks flit from their hollows

dressed for the day, with their laced gold tips

on black wings wavering from a branch—what fresh

entertainment, that the year's only snow should come

so late. The weather must have wanted,

                            as everyone does,

more gore. It must have longed to be newsworthy—

to be as astonishing as the moths, or as Jesus,

emerging out of some hollow, radiant and frail.

SECOND COMING

In March the grebe returns alone. He floats
past paddlings of mallards, shimming through

the common glossy necks and croaking calls.
Diving into the mucked-up flooded creek,

tiny, anonymous, but driven, he'll be at home
in larger, rougher waters. He hasn't come
to save us. He doesn't show me how to live

and so, in turn, I'll give no thought to how
he tilts his beak, feeling something watching,

or to how his red unsympathetic eye
must see me—plain, dumb, just loitering here.

MIGRATION

Wherever we would go, we cannot go there.

Here is the fact: the tundra swans know

where they are flying. Look at them,

their bodies barbing north, the stew

of cloud and dark not deterring

them on their way, long wings like dresses

flowered in wind, their voices like that,

falling and rising, far off, a fluted "who,"

not asking that: having, in their name,

a destination. Our families lounge

in cluttered rooms, wishing to be called

as birds are, with that kind of clarity, driving

to church, the bar, the shrink. This is why

we pray: we were not born tundra swans.

Look at them laughing, flapping over us,

thieves. Eyes skyward, we live this way,

plotting our wars, buying cars, weeping,

some days—hushed and watchful as the deaf.

THIS MUST BE HOW THE MONKS FELT ON THEIR WAY

to Castelmonte, heads lolling from their necks,

longing to leave their legs howling

on the uphill road.

From the weeds rise mosaics, the Stations of the Cross.

Here Jesus bleeds, his mouth black tile,

his eyes blooming white.

At the peak, the last mosaic's just gold squares,

the spirit's ascent.

The poplars clench the rock up here harder.

The smallest flowers keep drinking

from the soil, digging in their heels.

I'D SAY GOD

after Wordsworth

The kale seedlings, white torsos warped

to the grow light, coil their roots and wrest

strength from their traymates. They are at war,

as they must be, forgivably. A caterpillar works

the tomato plants in the field. Come closer. You can see

the white darts of wasp eggs shot into its body,

their spiny promise on the pillow of flesh.

The wasps are awake. Veil-winged,

ecstatic, they throb out, a birth hymn,

graze the air, then eat the caterpillar's body.

If I were walking here without a view for detail,

I might say it's peaceful—the sun over the hills

spitting heat, brooding pink on the beds.

The cattle dog with three legs hops by,

fleas communing on his ribs. He grins

in the dusk, ready to snap in the face of any cow.

If I saw him from the purslane farther off, I'd say God

was with him—though, like us, he'd never know.

CONVERSION

And sometimes after weeks of the doves, of drab

prophets in gray gowns who low and squeak up

with wings like ungreased wheels, this fervor comes—

the phoebes buzzing in tongues, finding ground

to feed—and soon the thickets trill

with transients and refugees, nesting, fluting.

The mind rebuilds its high places.

Sometimes the day brings clairvoyance,

the doves set to leave their trundled bodies—

as if they might burst, recant the skewed philosophy

they moaned from rooftops where they'd stayed,

belled and soft on shingle. Whatever it was in us,

sleeping, cracks and climbs out. Sometimes the grebes,

on their way north, land here, idling, before thrashing on.

HERE

on the curling grin of water teethed
through rock, gnawing this canyon, one's slung fast
with the rushing, that sound like theatergoers

when the play's half done, a rich-stirred babble fluming

white from the rounded stones, mergansers
needling up the other way, the lithe bottles of their bodies

flushed out, gunning against the pull

down here at the pant legs of the cliffs,
the cuffs of them frayed with bluets.
Prying to swerve past storm-downed limbs,

one becomes quick as an idea, as singular,

and is perfectly placid, as interested
in an afterlife as are the blackbirds winging up

to the sun-bleached trees.

How would one move outside of this?

Always some swallows razor skin off the water,

knifing the banks, their organs pumping,

one and more darting into their homes.

ARRIVAL

On some mornings you wake

having misplaced the self's blueprint,

and you wonder, what was my role? did I complain?

who loved me and when did this body come?

And you look at the squirrels' twisting haunches,

the roofs and wiry scrolling of the tops of trees,

the wearying pocked paint on the familiar barn

like feathers ruffed and molting,

and ask, how long will they stay?

The man who sets a lawn chair in the far field

apart from the dense curl of trees comes to mind;

how he has leaned through many noons,

dogless, without binoculars, without excuse

for choosing this place, a clash with the vacant plain

and still as slate. As you would join the squirrels

this morning, or be that soon storm-stripped paint,

wherever it goes, consider: what if we're granted glimpses

of the things we might, with work, become?

Let the man sit. Let him be unexplained.

LEAP

after Kierkegaard

There must be a joke in the light to lure him out—
though the sky droops, pewter and flat, the grim
first face of dawn—or he would not perch

in the spruce, launching into late winter

his red mantra. He sings like one of those doomsayers
on city streets, as urgent as that, only with a crimson
exuberance, an orange-mouthed sense. I wouldn't hope

to be a bird, but what about one of those

flea-like insects who show up on snow in March
hopping, plying themselves onto the bellies
of dogs and wool socks, whatever walks

and holds heat. The absurdity of their being

thrust into ice crystals too soon in spring—
such suffering, and for nothing but time
to make more sufferers before a departure

mired in pain, no doubt, headless and twitching—

it's stunning, that they jump sixty times their height

for a few dumb instants and sex. When the kingfisher

streaks past me upstream after some hoary

darting thing, then dives, terrible missile,

into the river's cadaverous crust, thrusting

far through the current then flashing out

wet-white-blue with that spiked crest

knifing the light and a fish in its thick

comic beak, I want that kind of faith

or unthinking willingness to fall

into the difficult places as cold and sure

as Abraham or as a simple tail feather

cued by the ancient stupidity we call

wisdom, and to be happy to go.

NOT LIKE GHOSTS BUT LIKE THE WHITE ROBES WORN

by deacons they glide into the flooded field tonight,

dark-beaked and substantial, folding down their wings.

Some dreamer standing in my place

might say God got sick of the moon and cut it up

with scissors, folding the pieces

into thousands of tundra swans, letting them

drift down to the breaking ice.

I have no fantasies—

they are plump and unholy, loaded up

with bone and blood and pipes

that allow, for the moment,

their thousand piccolo calls

and the mess that pours through them.

They are not winged men.

They are not robed. They have feet that churn mud,

icicles that claw rough feathers. More swans

are on their way, circling, glazing the trees, the spouts

of their necks stuck out of their bodies' foul tubs.

They call out. They are as irreverent as tin whistles,

unneedful of blessings, secular as calliopes. Listen.

They're piping loudest from the ground.

ABOUT THE AUTHOR

K. A. Hays is a native of southeast Pennsylvania. She read English literature at Bucknell and Oxford Universities and earned an MFA in the Literary Arts at Brown. Her poetry has appeared in such magazines as *Antioch Review*, *Gray's Sporting Journal*, *New Orleans Review*, *Northern Woodlands*, and *Southern Review*, and was selected by Natasha Tretheway for inclusion in *Best New Poets 2007*. She is also a fiction writer and verse translator whose work in those genres has appeared in *Gulf Coast*, *Cimarron Review*, *Hudson Review*, and other magazines. She lives in Lewisburg, Pennsylvania, where she holds the Emerging Writer Fellowship at Bucknell.

1997
Growing Darkness, Growing Light, Jean Valentine
Selected Poems, 1965-1995, Michael Dennis Browne
Your Rightful Childhood: New and Selected Poems, Paula Rankin
Headlands: New and Selected Poems, Jay Meek
Soul Train, Allison Joseph
The Autobiography of a Jukebox, Cornelius Eady
The Patience of the Cloud Photographer, Elizabeth Holmes
Madly in Love, Aliki Barnstone
An Octave Above Thunder: New and Selected Poems, Carol Muske

1998
Yesterday Had a Man In It, Leslie Adrienne Miller
Definition of the Soul, John Skoyles
Dithyrambs, Richard Katrovas
Postal Routes, Elizabeth Kirschner
The Blue Salvages, Wayne Dodd
The Joy Addict, James Harms
Clemency and Other Poems, Colette Inez
Scattering the Ashes, Jeff Friedman
Sacred Conversations, Peter Cooley
Life Among the Trolls, Maura Stanton

1999
Justice, Caroline Finkelstein
Edge of House, Dzvinia Orlowsky
A Thousand Friends of Rain: New and Selected Poems, 1976-1998,
        Kim Stafford
The Devil's Child, Fleda Brown Jackson
World as Dictionary, Jesse Lee Kercheval
Vereda Tropical, Ricardo Pau-Llosa
The Museum of the Revolution, Angela Ball
Our Master Plan, Dara Wier

2003
Imitation of Life, Allison Joseph
A Place Made of Starlight, Peter Cooley
The Mastery Impulse, Ricardo Pau-Llosa
Except for One Obscene Brushstroke, Dzvinia Orlowsky
Taking Down the Angel, Jeff Friedman
Casino of the Sun, Jerry Williams
Trouble, Mary Baine Campbell
Lives of Water, John Hoppenthaler

2004
Freeways and Aqueducts, James Harms
Tristimania, Mary Ruefle
Prague Winter, Richard Katrovas
Venus Examines Her Breast, Maureen Seaton
Trains in Winter, Jay Meek
The Women Who Loved Elvis All Their Lives, Fleda Brown
The Chronic Liar Buys a Canary, Elizabeth Edwards
Various Orbits, Thom Ward

2005
Laws of My Nature, Margot Schilpp
Things I Can't Tell You, Michael Dennis Browne
Renovation, Jeffrey Thomson
Sleeping Woman, Herbert Scott
Blindsight, Carol Hamilton
Fallen from a Chariot, Kevin Prufer
Needlegrass, Dennis Sampson
Bent to the Earth, Blas Manuel De Luna

2006
Burn the Field, Amy Beeder
Dog Star Delicatessen: New and Selected Poems 1979–2006,
        Mekeel McBride
The Sadness of Others, Hayan Charara
A Grammar to Waking, Nancy Eimers
Shinemaster, Michael McFee
Eastern Mountain Time, Joyce Peseroff
Dragging the Lake, Robert Thomas

2007
So I Will Till the Ground, Gregory Djanikian
Trick Pear, Suzanne Cleary
Indeed I Was Pleased With the World, Mary Ruefle
The Situation, John Skoyles
One Season Behind, Sarah Rosenblatt
The Playhouse Near Dark, Elizabeth Holmes
Drift and Pulse, Kathleen Halme
Black Threads, Jeff Friedman
On the Vanishing of Large Creatures, Susan Hutton

2008
The Grace of Necessity, Samuel Green
After West, James Harms
The Book of Sleep, Eleanor Stanford
Anticipate the Coming Reservoir, John Hoppenthaler
Parable Hunter, Ricardo Pau-Llosa
Convertible Night, Flurry of Stones, Dzvinia Orlowsky

2009
Divine Margins, Peter Cooley
Cultural Studies, Kevin Gonzalez
Cave of the Yellow Volkswagen, Maureen Seaton
Group Portrait from Hell, David Schloss
Birdwatching in Wartime, Jeffrey Thomson
Dear Apocalypse, K. A. Hays
Warhol-o-rama, Peter Oresick